How to Add a Device to My Amazon Account

Simple step-by-step instructions on All Devices and Apps

Corey Stone

including specific information will be considered an illegal act irrespective of if it is done electronically or in print. This extends to creating a secondary or tertiary copy of the work or a recorded copy and is only allowed with express written consent from the Publisher. All additional rights reserved.

The information in the following pages is broadly considered to be a truthful and accurate account of facts and as such any inattention, use or misuse of the information in question by the reader will render any resulting actions solely under their purview. There are no scenarios in which the publisher or the original author of this work can be in any fashion deemed liable for any hardship or damages that may befall them after undertaking information described herein.

Additionally, the information in the following pages is intended only for informational purposes and should thus be thought of as universal. As befitting its nature, it is presented without assurance regarding its prolonged validity or interim quality. Trademarks that are mentioned are done without written consent and can in no way be considered an endorsement from the trademark holder.

TABLE OF CONTENTS

Introduction

Did you purchase a new device? Do you wish to view your already purchased content on this device?

You will need an account to register in your device. Without an account, you cannot download any content. If you do not have one, then create. It is easy enough to do, as long as you know where to look.

You will discover the steps to ensuring you can access your Amazon content from any tablet, Kindle, or app you own.

You can select the correct chapter based on the device you purchased.

The steps are outlined to make it as easy as possible for you. Remember, you need to first set up your device with the network and internet connections before you can register with Amazon.

Again, you need an Amazon account. Or if you already have one, you can choose to upgrade it by paying for Prime to obtain access to movies and TV.

You can also purchase individual shows, movies, books, and other content without upgrading to Prime, Kindle Unlimited, Audible, or Amazon music.

The key is to have a free account to log in and begin registering your new device.

Chapter 1: How to Add a Device to Your Amazon Account

You need to have an account to begin. If you do not have, log onto Amazon.com, and follow the prompts for registering an email and password for an Amazon account.

You also need to make sure the device is connected to the internet.

1. Start the device.
2. Locate Amazon, either through a browser and going to Amazon.com or the app on the device.
3. From home, tap the menu button.
4. Open settings.

5. Find Amazon.

6. Open the app.

7. Tap log in or My Account.

8. In Amazon's "My Account," you will enter your username and password.

9. It will automatically register the new device when you log in.

If you need an Amazon account, just select "Create Account." This option allows you to establish a username and password. You can also name your device during the setup. You can do it later from your online account via the "manage your content and devices" section.

Chapter 2: How to Add a Fire Tablet to Your Amazon Account

If necessary, connect your device to the internet before you begin. You may need to walk through the setup for your tablet if you have not done so yet.

1. From the home screen on your tablet, open the app.
2. Swipe down on the Amazon home screen and tap more.
3. You will see "my account."
4. Select it.
5. Click register.
6. Enter your username and password.

Then, you're done.

If you do not have an account, you will need to "create account," setting up a new account and then follow the registration process for the device.

Chapter 3: How to Add a Fire TV to Your Amazon Account

Your TV is new, so once you make it through the TV set up and access an Internet connection, you can go to the Amazon app or Amazon.com.

1. Choose settings on the Fire TV menu.
2. Go to "My Account."
3. You can select "register."
4. Enter your log-in details.
5. Give your device a name.

You are ready to use your Amazon account for books, and if you have a prime account, you can use it for movies and other options.

Chapter 4: How to Add a PC to Your Amazon Account

Make sure the computer is connected to the Internet.

1. Your computer may have a Kindle for PC app. If it does, open the App.
2. Click on Tools.
3. Click Options.
4. Select "Register."
5. Enter your Amazon username and password.
6. Select the "Register" button to finish the setup.
7. You can now see all your Kindle content.

You can also go through a web browser.

1. Open a web browser.

2. Go to Amazon.com.

3. Log-in.

4. Select the drop-down menu under "account and lists."

5. You can view your devices, apps, and subscriptions.

6. Your PC, when registered with an Amazon account will appear.

7. If it does not, all you need to do is make a purchase and download to your "device," selecting your PC.

It is easier to use the Kindle for PC app, but you can also view things in the cloud reader from a browser.

Chapter 5: How to Add an Android Device to Your Amazon Account

Make sure the device is connected to Wi-Fi or your network.

1. Find the Amazon app on your Android device.
2. Most devices will already have it saved to the "home screen."
3. If it is not, go to the app area.
4. Find Amazon.
5. Open it.
6. Enter your log-in details.
7. The device is now registered.

Chapter 6: How to Add an iOS Device to Your Amazon Account

Make sure the iOS device is on the net or network signal.

1. From the device, select the Amazon app.

2. Enter your account username and password.

3. Sign in.

4. Your Kindle library will appear.

5. You can give a name to your device, so you know which one it is. Enter your online account, selecting "your devices," and then edit from the actions tab.

Conclusion

Adding a device to your Amazon account is easy. As you read above, for the different devices, you need to open the app, log-in, and register the device.

The minute you download a book or content to your device, it automatically registers in it.

You may see an option, such as 1, 2, 3, or 4 as the device names, but you can change that by going online via a web browser and into the device list, renaming all the devices.

Thank you for downloading *"How to Add a Device to My Amazon Account: Simple step-by-*

step instructions on All Devices and Apps," please leave a review if you enjoyed the content.

Thank you!

Check Out Other Books

Please go here to check out other books that might interest you:

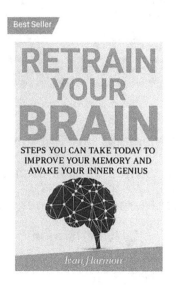

Retrain Your Brain: Steps You Can Take Today
to Improve Your Memory and Awake Your
Inner Genius by Ivan Harmon

Enhance Memory: Find Out How Memory Functions, Switch On Your Brain and Have Better Memory - two-book bundle by Ivan Harmon

Boost Your Brain Power: Learn Better, Smarter,

and faster - Scientifically Proven Guides to

Sharpen Your Focus and Retrain Your Brain

by Ivan Harmon

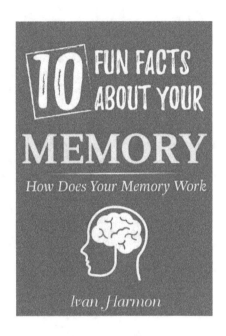

10 Fun Facts About Your Memory

by Ivan Harmon

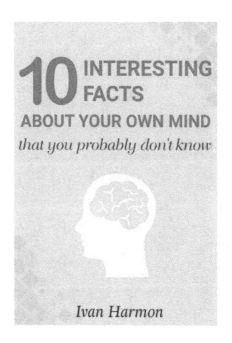

10 Interesting Facts About Your Own Mind that

You Probably Don't Know

by Ivan Harmon

Switch On Your Brain: 10 Fun and Interesting Facts About Your Own Mind that You Want to Know by Ivan Harmon

Memory Exercises: Create a habit for memory enhancement by Ivan Harmon

Have Better Memory: Your Memory How It Works and How to Improve It by Ivan Harmon

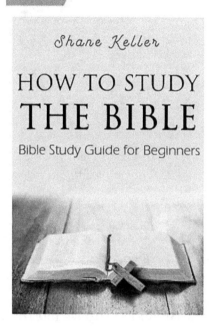

How to Study the Bible: Bible Study Guide for Beginners by Shane Keller

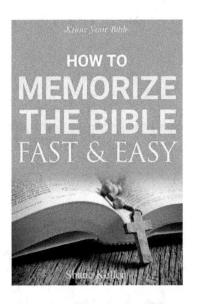

Know your Bible: How to Memorize the Bible

Fast and Easy

by Shane Keller

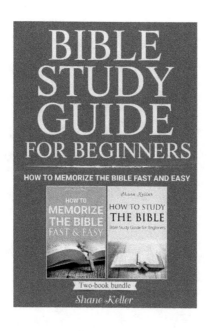

Bible Study Guide for Beginners: How to

Memorize the Bible Fast and Easy

by Shane Keller

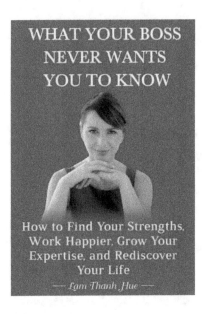

What Your Boss Never Wants You to Know:

How to Find Your Strengths, Work Happier,

Grow Your Expertise, and Rediscover Your Life

by Lam Thanh Hue

ISBN 9781981955596

90000 >